M000248812

I ♥ MY TRUCK

DEDICATION

To Joanna, without whom none of this
would have happened.

—W.S.

In memory of Wally Hottel, a true truck drivin' man,
and all the good times we shared while driving
our Diamond Reo.

—R.S.

Published by Ronnie Sellers Productions, Inc.

Copyright © 2005 Ronnie Sellers Productions, Inc.
Photography Copyright © 2005 William Bennett Seitz
All rights reserved.

President & Publisher: Ronnie Sellers
Publishing Director: Robin Haywood
Managing Editor: Mary Baldwin
Designer: George Corsillo, Design Monsters

See permissions and credits on page 94

81 West Commercial St., Portland, Maine 04101
For ordering information:
Phone: 1-800-625-3386
Visit our Web site: www.rsvp.com
email: rsp@rsvp.com

ISBN: 1-56906-594-2

I ♥ MY TRUCK

A TRIBUTE TO
THE GREAT AMERICAN
PICKUP TRUCK

Photography by WILLIAM BENNETT SEITZ

Ronnie Sellers Productions, Portland, Maine

INTRODUCTION

They asked me to write something to get this truck book started.

Use both hands on the door handle. Yank her hard. Won't open without some coaxing. Let the dog jump in. Climb in halfway amd give the gas a few kicks. Pause, then hit the ignition. Let the starter crank a few times, then give her a rest. Pet the dog. Scrape some frost off the inside of the windshield. Give her another crank. Feel the chassis shake as she rumbles out of her sleep. Her first few turns are stiff, uneven. Then she straightens out. The shaking stops. Goose her a little to say good morning. Pull the door closed hard. Turn on the radio and drop her into gear. Push the dog over and let up on the clutch. You're rolling. Smell the oil burning off of the block. Sweet. Don't bother with the heat. Not going far enough for it to work anyway. Let the dog stick his head out of his window. Watch his ears lift in the breeze. Open her up a little. The tires whine. Shift into high gear. The engine relaxes. Roll down your window and take in some fresh air yourself.

They'd laugh at you if you told them how much you love your truck. Some love affairs are best kept to yourself.

– Ronnie Sellers

I LOVE MY TRUCK

by Drew Rozell

Last night I went for a walk around the property through the open hardwoods, on a hill above ancient farm country . . . I found myself back at the house, staring at my truck in the driveway. Understand that I love my truck. I love climbing into it. I love driving it. I love seeing it in a parking lot and knowing it's mine.

The truck still bears Washington state plates, the ones with Mt. Rainier right in the middle.

I began thinking about the man I bought it from. When I was searching for a vehicle, I ended up looking at exactly one truck (it was perfect). I liked the man selling this vehicle and he liked me. Days later his vehicle passed on to me. We connected.

• 1954 CHEVROLET 3100

THE ULTIMATE SOCIAL NECESSITY

by John L. Braese

Most of my questions on animal care and husbandry have been answered sitting in the middle of a dirt road, old pickup doors handle to handle with farmers sitting inside. I have traded more seeds, recipes, and ideas sitting in the parking lot of the feed store in my old pickup than I have ever found in any publication . . . You meet the neighbors by walking to their house and asking for a pull home when the old pickup truck breaks down. Don't worry, you will reciprocate the favor when their old pickup truck breaks down. Your old pickup pulling their old pickup (or vice versa) cements a bond between the two of you. And finally, I really feel at peace with myself and this lifestyle when I'm sitting on the tailgate, out in the field about sundown after a hard day's work, just me and my old pickup.

• CHEVROLET CIRCA 1950

REAL FINE LOVE

Lyrics by John Hiatt

Well I never went to college, babe
I did not have the luck
I rolled out of Indiana in the
  back of a pickup truck.

• 1949 DODGE B-1

THE TRUCK SONG

Lyrics by Lyle Lovett

**Turn down that highway
Turn up that dirt road
It's over three days
Since I left Houston
Old Black's my truck's name
She's held together
By B.F. Goodtire
And bailing wire.**

• 1950 FORD

OLD PICKUP TRUCK

by Marvin West

Monday through Saturday, this is a working truck, even in the holiday season. It hauls a giant load of debris or enough bricks to make the springs sag. It hauls wheelbarrows and heavy scaffolding and five-gallon paint buckets and a variety of tools. Sometimes it hauls away trimmings from our modest courtyard garden. Best I can tell, the old pickup truck never complains.

● 1949 INTERNATIONAL KB-2

PARK THE PICKUP, KISS THE GIRL

Lyrics by David Berg, Annie Tate, and Sam Tate

Find a spot with a pretty view
Pull her over next to you
The whole world's your oyster
She's your pearl
Now park the pickup, kiss the girl.

• 1955 CHEVROLET 3100

ODE TO PICKUP TRUCKS

by Taylor Wilson

There have been times in my life when I have been caught without a pickup truck and, looking back on it, I kind of remember feeling naked. . . . Man, when I was a kid and an aspiring outdoorsman, a pickup truck could be something like a treasure chest. See a group of men standing around looking in the bed of a pickup truck and who knew what wonders were likely to be held within? Depending on the season, there could be all kinds of outdoor objects of desire in the back of trucks − things like big bucks, coolers of fish, or perhaps even a timber rattler that had the misfortune of receiving death by skid marks.

• 1949 FORD F-1

I'd like to lay this old hammer down
Drive my pickup truck to town
Find a friend and just hang around.

• 1959 CHEVROLET FLEETSIDE

MUD ON THE TIRES

Lyrics by Brad Paisley and Charles Dubois

There's a place I know about, where the dirt road runs out
We can try out the four-wheel drive
Come on now whata' ya say? Girl I can hardly wait
To get a little mud on the tires.

• 1946 HALF-TON DODGE

THEY STILL DO THAT

by Dave P. Fisher

For the benefit of those among us who remain so unaware,
Yes, cowboys are still on the range and not exactly rare . . .
The work is still as hard and hasn't changed that much,
But a few things make it easier like pickup trucks and such.

IN THE MARKET
FOR A MAN?

by Lee Pitts

The best way to judge a man is by looking at his pickup truck.

• 1938 STUDEBAKER COUPE

A FRONT ROW SEAT TO HEAR OLE JOHNNY SING

Lyrics by Shel Silverstein

All I wanted all my life
Was a TV set and a truck and a wife
And a front row seat to hear ole Johnny sing.

• 1936 FORD 830

MY TRUCK IS YELLOW

by Ronnie

My truck is yellow
The dash is blue
I like my truck
a lot more than you.

• 1948 FORD F-1

MY HUSBAND, A CITY BOY, DECIDES TO BUY A TRUCK

by Debra Marquart

This is the new truck, he says. Gone
are the days of gun racks and roped deer,
tires kicking up tufts of dirt, the dark
shrinking silhouette of a cowboy hat
as the truck climbs the last rise. For me,
it was hay bales, straw bales, alfalfa bales,
rocks, rocks, and more rocks, cranky
stick-shifts, slippery clutches, feet barely
reaching the pedals, driving lunch out
to Dad in the August fields, dust and sweat
slicked seats, the smell of oil and tractor
grease, the thunk and tumble of gas cans
rolling in the back.

• 1956 INTERNATIONAL S-120

A GIRL WHO DRIVES
A PICKUP TRUCK

by Rich Wayland

Now she ain't afraid to go her own way
And drive off the beaten path
If the road gets rocky if the road gets rough
She ain't the kind to turn back
When she goes by drivin' like a thunderbolt of lightnin'
I feel like my heart's been struck
'Cause I'm crazy 'bout a girl, a certain kind of girl
A girl who drives a pickup truck.

• 1950 INTERNATIONAL HARVESTER

MY GRANDDADDY WAS KING

by Michael Baxter

"Take me home with you. Take me home now," she flirted shamelessly, metal flakes sparkling in the bright sunlight. Though relatively petite in size by Texas standards, this little pickup was just what I had been looking for. Her smooth, nostalgic lines and flared sides reminded me of a smaller version of the truck that my granddaddy Owens had driven for so many years. He'd pick me up after school, and after tossing my "grip" into the cab, he'd help me climb in to sit beside him on that big bench seat for the trip to his place way out in the "country." Bouncing along back roads in that dusty old truck was much more of an adventure than riding in our family's Ford Fairlane or the Rambler to Crook's Foodtown. It allowed me the opportunity to look down on the world from a totally different perspective . . . the perspective of a little kid riding in a big truck. I was King of the Road. Well, more like Prince of the Road. Because when we were in that truck, my granddaddy was King.

• 1950 GMC

HONKY TONKER

Lyrics by Steve Forbert

Well, every evening when the news is over
And the moon is a climbing high
I crank up my old pickup truck
And baby, down the road I fly.

• 1939 CHEVROLET

COWBOYS ARE MY WEAKNESS

Lyrics by Chris Waters, Tom Shapiro, and
Holly Dunn

I really go for a rodeo Romeo
I gotta know what's under that hat
Show me a man who loves his old pickup truck
You gotta love somebody like that.

• 1955 FORD F-100

AMERICAN PIE

Lyrics by Don McLean

**I was a lonely teenage broncin' buck
With a pink carnation and a pickup truck.**

• 1954 FORD F-100

LOVE TOUGH AS A PICKUP TRUCK

Lyrics by Jim Witter

I need a love tough as a pickup truck
And two arms that are strong enough
To hold on tight through a Texas wind
Stick around 'til the end.

I need a kiss sweet as honey from a bee
A touch as soft as a summer breeze
I need a love, love - love - love
Tough as a pickup truck.

PICKUP TRUCK CAFÉ

Lyrics by Brenn Hill

Down at the Pickup Truck Café
We drink coffee here every day
We sit and talk the morning away
Down at the Pickup Truck Café.

• 1940 INTERNATIONAL K-1 AND 1948 DIAMOND T

HARD WORKIN' TRUCK

Lyrics by James Coffey

I'm lean, I'm mean,
I'm a workin' machine
Getting it all done is just routine
Climbing through the mud, stone,
Dirt, and muck
I'm a hard workin' truck.

• DODGE CIRCA 1950

A HUNDRED AND ONE

Lyrics by Kye Fleming, Rich Wayland, and
Mary Ann Kennedy

**Tommy still drives that ol' pickup truck
He had back in high school
He says he won't trade it in
'Cause they don't make 'em like they used to.**

• 1933 DODGE

ALL AMERICAN COUNTRY BOY

Lyrics by Keith Stegall and Charlie Craig

I drive a pickup truck and I don't pass the buck
And I always speak my mind
I'm hooked on TV, Rolaids, and b.c.'s
And I know how to have a good time
I'm a little bit rowdy and a little bit tame
Ain't no way I'm ever gonna change.

• 1952 INTERNATIONAL L-110

PICKUP MAN

Lyrics by Kerry Kurt Phillips and Howard Perdew

You can set my truck on fire, roll it down a hill
But I still wouldn't trade it for a Coupe DeVille
It's got an eight-foot bed that never
  has to be made
You know, if it weren't for trucks we wouldn't
  have tailgates
I met all my wives in traffic jams
You know there's something women like
  about a Pickup Man.

• 1955 STUDEBAKER E-7

WHEELS OF FORTUNE

by John Spong

Pickups are where we first learned to drive and then to break curfew, where we were able to play the stereo as loud as we wanted, make attempts to get nearer to the opposite sex, and dream of one day getting out on our own.

• 1929 FORD STREET ROD

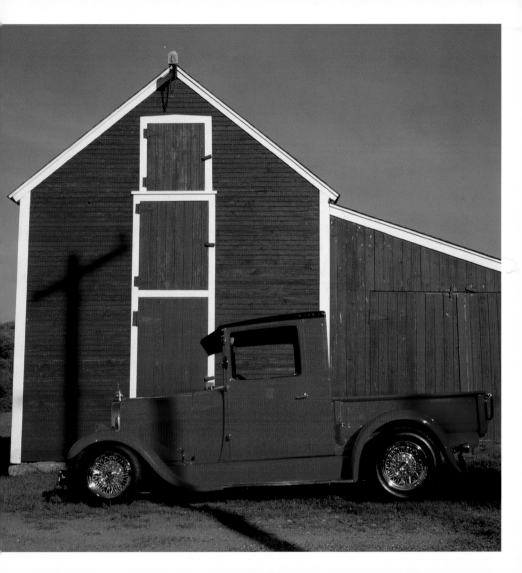

VACANT LOT

by Regis Auffray

Behind the tenements
the vacant lot
abounds in life and adventure . . .

There
the old pickup truck
rusty
musty interior
yet with enough shine
for a sleek and swift spaceship.

• 1945 CHEVROLET

PICKUP TRUCK SONG

Lyrics by Jerry Jeff Walker

Yea, I used to look forward to Saturdays
When me and my grandpa'd get away
We'd hop in his pickup truck and we'd go to town
We had a couple chores that we had to do
It didn't take long before we were through
Then we'd let the pickup truck just wander around.

• 1950 GMC

CAB OF MY TRUCK

Lyrics by Brett Beavers, Dierks Bentley,
and Mark Eugene Nessler

Four wheels turnin'
Two hearts burnin'
We go runnin' wild
Gonna make a million
Memories for every hundred
Thousand miles
Learnin' everything I'll ever need
To know about life and love
In the cab of my truck.

• 1953 CHEVROLET DELUXE 3600

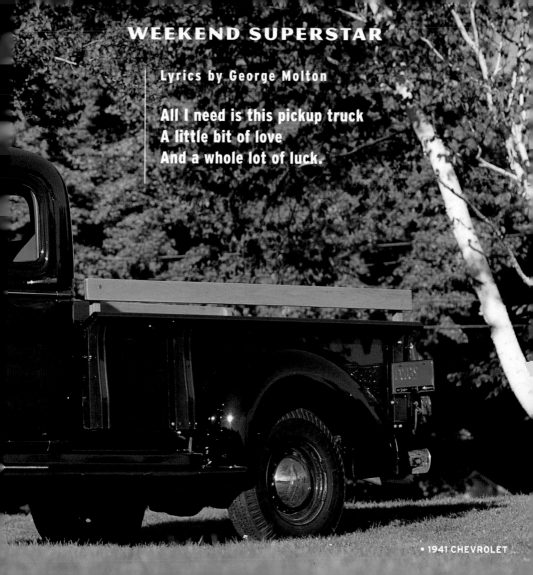

WEEKEND SUPERSTAR

Lyrics by George Molton

All I need is this pickup truck
A little bit of love
And a whole lot of luck.

• 1941 CHEVROLET

KICK IT UP

Lyrics by Jim Robinson and Andy Byrd

Punch the clock on party time
Jamming this old pickup across the county line
Ain't it good to be alive.

NO ORDINARY MAN

Lyrics by Lonnie Williams, Frank Dycus,
and Tracy Byrd

He climbs into that old pickup
Black coffee in his hand
Rodeo ain't no ordinary life
But a cowboy ain't no ordinary man.

• 1958 CHEVROLET FLEETSIDE

A BELOVED COMPANION NEARS THE END OF THE ROAD

by Mark W. Mayfield

It's finally happening. After 218,000 miles, my trusty ol' pickup truck is running out of time. . . . I've tried to prepare myself for this inevitable day. But right now, I can't think of anything except the great times we shared. I remember how she purred with pleasure when I shifted her into overdrive for the first time. I remember that funny face she made whenever I loaded her bed with horse manure. Several years ago, her playful mood suddenly turned somber. Out of the blue, she began to talk about "the end of the road." She made me promise that I would never allow her to suffer needlessly. She begged me to someday park her under her favorite tree and permanently disconnect her spark plugs. How could I refuse her request? She was a heavenly vision of moonlit loveliness. She was the most beautiful truck on the road, and I would've promised her anything.

• 1937 MACK JR.

TRUCK JOKE

Anonymous

A rancher from Texas, eager to impress a farmer from Maine, explains, "I get into my truck first thing in the morning and it takes me two full hours just to reach my southern boundary. Then, if I turn east, it takes me three hours to reach the eastern-most point. If I keep going and drive all the way around my land, I won't get back home until after dark."

Unimpressed, the Mainer looks at him and replies, "Ayuh. I've got a truck like that, too."

MY KINDA TRUCK

by Baxter Black

Pickups are kinda like welding gloves.
The pockmarks are part of the deal.
Not pretty, just built to get the job done.
Like the dummy behind the wheel.

• 1941 DODGE WC-1

SANTA'S GONNA COME IN A PICKUP TRUCK

Lyrics by Don Rich and Red Simpson

Santa can't bring his reindeer
He'll leave them far away
But don't you worry 'bout him
He's gonna be here Christmas day
He's got a big red pickup
With four-wheel drive and all
And there's gonna be a Merry Christmas
A Merry Christmas for all.

•1946 DODGE WC

MY FIRST TRUCK

by Rick Schwolsky

My first truck was a lot like my first girlfriend; high maintenance. She (the truck) was a classic old red International with big wheel fenders, springs popping up through the seat cushions, and a one-station radio that made country-western songs sound even sadder than they really were. She shifted hard and it took two strong men to steer her around a corner. I put a lot of energy into that darned old thing, and kept her running strong and looking good. Somehow she made me feel like a man. It would take another decade before I could truly say the same thing about a woman.

• 1949 INTERNATIONAL KB-2

GOODBYE, OLD BLUE

by John Sater

A few days ago I had to drive down around Sandpoint to see a man I've known for quite a few years. He heard me drive in and came out on his porch. The first words he said were, "Where is your old pickup?"

I had to tell him the sad story of how Old Blue finally had to be turned out to pasture. He seemed genuinely sad. My old pickup was so much a part of my existence. It seems odd to be maudlin over such a thing as an inanimate piece of metal. But it was more than that. It was like a special friend. As it got along in years it developed signs of old age. It's hard to see an old friend going downhill and know there is really nothing you can do to prolong its life. When I finally had to retire it I nearly felt I should dig a hole and bury it or at least hold a memorial service for it. That's the least I could do.

• 1951 CHEVROLET

OLD PICKUP TRUCK HAULED NOSTALGIA

by Linda Wuebben

My husband, Bob, and I were never impressed with a pickup as a status symbol. When we contracted to buy the farm in 1980, along with it came the family pickup. It was a cherry red Ford, and it could barrel with the best of them. Its main purpose was to haul hogs to market. Nothing pretty about that. . . .

How many laws did we break in that well-loved vehicle? There were never enough seat belts nor were any used. No one ever fell off the back end on our evening romps, but of course, we weren't traveling 60 miles an hour and didn't have any place to go.

But the memories! The times we spent together in that red beater forged a family bond, which we will hold dear in our hearts, and none of us will ever forget. After all, it isn't the color or style, or size. Family – isn't that what matters most?

• 1955 FORD F-100

VEGAS

Lyrics by Shel Silverstein

Baby . . . we're gonna go to Vegas
Win more money than you've ever seen
Far as this pick-up truck and
  forty-eight bucks will take us.

• 1941 STUDEBAKER

MISUNDERSTOOD SIGNALS

by Barbara Bockelman

The only time a pickup won't start
Is when you're running late.

• 1939 FORD 92-D

PICKUPS HOLD MANY MEMORIES

by Loran Smith

Not sure when it will come about, but one of these days, I am going to own a pickup. I want a used one, too. I know it is not likely, but I would like one that has a gearshift in the floor – for sentimental reasons. The first vehicle in our family – that I remember – was a used pickup. I can remember how proud my daddy was to own his own truck. It's hard to farm without a pickup.

As time went by, the old pickup was replaced by a new one, and that was special. But along came those high school years and you get your driver's license. Then you begin thinking about asking someone for a date. Not many girls wanted to go out with a guy who came calling in a pickup.

No matter, I am going to get that truck someday. I realize, too, while times have changed, I still won't be able to make any dates.

Besides, I wouldn't want to lose my pickup truck in a divorce case.

• 1950 CHEVROLET 3600

PEOPLE LIKE US

**Lyrics by David Lee Murphy
and Kim Tribble**

**'Cause of people like us
there's honky tonk music,
long neck bottles,
rusty old pickup trucks. . . .**

• 1941 FORD 11-C

A REAL PICKUP MAN

by James W. Dolan

Like a workhorse, a truck waits patiently to be called upon to undertake another task; ever ready to be of service. Only those that have listened for the call of the wild or have dreamed of leaping into the saddle and heading West can appreciate the truck owner's gritty sense of independence and self-sufficiency.

Credits